On the Bottom

Also by Stuart Friebert

POETRY

Dreaming of Floods *Calming Down* *Up in Bed*
Stories My Father Can Tell *Uncertain Health* *The Darmstadt Orchids*
Funeral Pie *Near Occasions of Sin* *Speak Mouth to Mouth* *Floating Heart*
Kein Trinkwasser *Die Prokuristen kommen* *Nicht Hinauslehnen*

PROSE

Der Gast, und sei er noch so schlecht
The Language of the Enemy

TRANSLATIONS

Günter *Eich: Valuable Nail: Selected Poems* (with David Young & David Walker)
Karl Krolow: On Account Of: Selected Poems
Miroslav Holub: *Sagittal Section* (with Dana Habová)
Giovanni Raboni: *The Coldest Year of Grace* (with Vinio Rossi)
Marin Sorescu: *Hands Behind My Back* (with Gabriela Dragnea & Adriana Varga)
Karl Krolow: *What'll We Do With This Life?: Selected Poems*
Judita Vaičiūnaitė: *Fire, Put Out By Fire: Selected Poems (*with Viktoria Skrupskelis)
Sylva Fischerová: *The Swing in the Middle of Chaos: Selected Poems*
(with the author)
Sylva Fischerová: *Stomach of the Soul: Selected Poems*
*(*with the author & A.J. Hauner)
Karl Krolow: *Puppets in the Wind: Selected Poems*
Kuno Raeber: *Be Quiet: Selected Poems*

ANTHOLOGIES

A Field Guide to Contemporary Poetry & Poetics (with David Young & David Walker)
The Longman Anthology of Contemporary American Poetry (with David Young)
Models of the Universe: An Anthology of the Prose Poem (with David Young)

TEXTBOOK

Max Frisch: Als der Krieg zu Ende war

On the Bottom

Poems

Stuart Friebert

Iris Press
Oak Ridge, Tennessee

Design: Robert B. Cumming, Jr.

Library of Congress Cataloging-in-Publication Data

Friebert, Stuart, 1931-
[Poems. Selections]
On the bottom : poems / Stuart Friebert.
pages ; cm
ISBN 978-1-60454-231-8 (softcover : acid-free paper)
I. Title.
PS3556.R48A6 2015
811'.54—dc23

2015026144

Acknowledgments

Great thanks to the editors of these journals, in which some of the poems appeared, sometimes in slightly different form:

Agni, Chaminade Literary Review, Chariton Review, Comstock Review, Denver Quarterly, Great River Review, Hampden-Sydney Poetry Review, Home Planet News, Lalitamba, Mirmar, The Miser, Offcourse, Pinyon Review, Pittsburgh Quarterly, Plume, Poet Lore, Pudding, Queen's Quarterly, Rattle, Red Wheelbarrow, Talking River, 10x3 plus, Voyages, West Branch

North River Press published a limited edition broadside of "Courtship."

For KAZU / that's who!

Contents

1 A Few Shadows

Casting • 15
Proximodistal • 16
"When There's Just One of You Left" • 17
Madonnas • 18
Good Lord • 20
Some Sun on Cloud Tops • 21
Courtship • 22
Terminal Tackle • 23
Lake of the Ozarks • 24
Mother, Fishing • 26
Bitter End • 28
The Titanic's Hold •
Absent Flag • 30
Wash-Hole • 31
The Armur River • 32
"A Hideous Thing to Find in the Heart of the Continent" • 33
Pesticating • 34
Job's Tears • 35
Ithuriel's Spear • 36
Meat-in-the-Pot • 37
Third and Galena • 38
Gone to Sleep • 39

2 Shedding Thoughts

Hallux • 43
Water Ouzel • 44
Cleptoparisitic • 45
Birds of Paradise • 47
Tucotuco • 48
Tom, Dick & Harry • 49
Sea Squirt • 50

Hammerheads • 51
Meerkat • 52
Milksnake • 53
Spiders in Winter • 54
Cougars Kill People • 55
Surplus Killing • 56
Beast of Kings • 57
Everything Else • 58
Stotting • 60

3 Not Everything's Always Clear

Flying Wedding Rings • 63
Sow Cat • 64
Golden Bees • 65
Brief Reflection on Weapons • 66
"Large Sturgeon Caught with Iron Cross in Its Stomach" • 67
Crook Nose Jack McCall • 68
"Lonesome Charley" • 69
A Wrestler Named Plato • 70
Love of Science • 71
Precipitazione Dall'alto • 72
"A Single Quantum of Visible Light" • 73
Spaghettification • 74
Supraoral • 75
Brief Reflection on the Black 6 Mouse • 77
Seeing the Elephant • 79
"Two Great Minds Afloat" • 80
Kornjuden • 81
The Last Mattress • 82
Death-Qualified • 83
Supersedure • 84

I

A Few Shadows

Casting

Have you ever seen someone grow younger,
more fully alive, after turning away from

something done passionately, obsessively,
early in life, to something so different,

which begins on a cold white table, where
a body lies motionless like an anchor, its

limbs imprisoned in a sheath of pain until
you study the X-ray, cut down into the dark

blue swells and things calm down? No? Why,
it's not that at all, you say? Well, what then?

Proximodistal

—for Sarah

Meaning the fetus develops from the minuscule,
elongated mass of cells along the neural groove,

which will morph into a solid spinal column if all
goes well. When we provide sustenance the next

ever so many years, is that nothing? I'm walking
in the garden with my daughter, explaining why

some of the bushes aren't doing well. She bends
to wattle them with her fingers. She's such a quiet

little girl of late, her hair sticking to her temples,
wet with perspiration. We know she has thoughts

and feelings we're not capable of sensing yet, if
ever. Suddenly she catches a butterfly I'd not seen,

its wings powdering her palms. I want to say, please
let it go, but her eyes dwell on it with such tenderness

I know it'll spread its wings wide again soon. Well,
she says putting it back on the leaf, I'd like to play tea-

time now, takes me by the hand to pull me back toward
the house. I ought to tell her, I… My cheeks flush, she

goes quicker & quicker, while I long to rest, go slower
& slower, somewhat scared now, thrown off balance, rub

my chest with my free hand, till she graduates from med
school and gives me a stethoscope for listening to the past.

"When There's Just One of You Left"

she says, "I'll call every day," a daughter
you wouldn't want to do without. Lately,

I'm worried by all sorts of questions, but
she says, "One at a time, daddio, breathe

in, breathe out, which I do so there's no
need for the little brown sack to breathe

into, CO^2 to the rescue. My father would
rush me to the shower, steam up the whole

house till my lungs relaxed and the house
could return to its normal tensions. He who

had saved me lay dying in a modern spital
whose doctors refused him more morphine.

Along came the daughter you wouldn't want
to do without, by then a doctor herself: "At 93,

gentlemen, my grandpa's not likely to become
addicted, now is he?" I'd wanted to slap them silly,

might have if she hadn't just entered, a serious look
in her eyes. For the most part, she does everything

in silence, before she sets to work to right another
wrong. It is now very late, and it's better to cut this

short. If you come this way, you'd do well to let her
have a look at you. Meanwhile, the best of health!

Madonnas

—for Diane

1 Portrait Madonnas

She usually appears as a half-length figure
against solid gold leaf, often with cherubs
around her blue robe, starred in turn with
gold, sometimes draped over her quiet head.

In Italy's oldest churches, she's dark and
fair, as tall as you, but like women who've
never worked, there's something of a melancholy
over her brow, as if she'd dread to give birth
again; but then there's that moment, her eyes
looking away, a door perhaps ajar at the end
of a hallway, God's head filling the opening.

2 Madonna Enthroned

She's sitting on a throne or elevated platform,
with harpies or saints around her, never both.
I can't look, she seems to be saying, and she's
turning her hand round and round as if she were
playing a game. Her cheeks have lost some bloom.

If the Devil appeared, she'd get right down and
run to God. "But we're the family of – the boy,"
she'd exclaim. "And it's your place to protect us."
A faint doubt crosses her eyes, "Were we doing
right?" she wonders. "Let him have my place,
you won't miss me." The fever-wind subsides.

3 Madonna in the Sky

It's like starting a new life up there, living
in a bigger house, Heaven suggested as a circle,

or halo of light, and clouds floating round about.
Just above the ground, where she'd be lost of
course, some cherubs seem to be carrying on.
In the earliest paintings, the glory surrounds
her entirely, nicely oval, but her eyes seem
dead, as if she were glad to be out of sight.
She'd be more relieved if we looked away.

4 *Pastoral Madonna*

As you'd expect, the background's pure landscape,
sometimes just bare rocks or roses, but more often
there's an entire garden, and she's the gardener,
wrought-iron shears at her belt. The scents of blooms
around her, that mysterious aid to memory, revives me.
But what's this, in the little frame in the hall of the inn,
she's talking to an angel who seems concerned about
a scratch on her face. I wash my hands, and through
the window over the sink, some miles distant, there's
a steep stone wall rising way up over the Rhone valley.

5 *Madonna in the House*

These are the fewest in number, by Northern painters
who were happiest at home, it seems. Look, there she
is in a Flemish bedroom, as if she had nothing very nice
to tell you about herself. And there, at the carpenter's,
a knot in the string around her finger, her rosary of tiny
beads crying out, May the Holy Ghost be with you!
In another, she's gossiping about the infant Jesus to
a neighbor lady, "He'll be coming home soon, muddy
again no doubt, so I better fix his supper." And in one
we own, over the bed in the back bedroom, she's
helping herself to the one perfect chocolate in a dirty
brown box. "We're either going up to Bethlehem next
season, or down to the seashore to watch the men fish,"
she seems to be saying, "But I just don't know for sure."

Good Lord

You probably know that all animals
above the so-called lowest emerge
from eggs of one sort or another—
some inside the mother's body, as in
most mammals, but most outside, which
must of course contain enough food
to develop and hence run larger, often
in such colorations and markings that
Gauguin once said, "Good Lord!"
(ramming his brush into his hands).
"I was ready for these blessed birds
but the insolence of such color? Never!"

Van Gogh was firing off his pistol
at the time, looking intently into his
own wild eyes, and to calm down took
up the sand grouse's egg, shaped like
a cylinder, a gift from Gauguin, which
he slowly turned over and over until
it unnerved him; and he ran to that bed
in the corner, pulled the covers up over
everything but one eye, drifting in and out
of troubled sleep, vowing to crack open
his head like an egg if Gauguin so much
as mentioned that thing about his ear.

Some Sun on Cloud Tops

For some, Hopper-minded, an image
of extreme loneliness. For me, a sign

to sharpen dull hooks, drink at least two
Labatt's and appear well pleased, even if

I'm weeks now into cabining on this island,
the fishing the poorest in many a summer,

the blueberries late so the bears are coming
closer, the last golden eagle overhead unable

to scare the flock of gulls off far enough for
its customarily larger share of fry, both eyes

squeezed in as if to say, *I'm to blame, relax.*
So I do, before heading down to bail the boat

out, yank the cord hard to start the balky motor.
The lake's perfect in the half-shade, the sun

mercifully deciding to stay hidden just enough
to keep the water murky with dark clouds, wind

chopping the surface so nothing alive below can
see me casting now. Hopper, I read, also liked to

fish alone; and he'd sit down at the end of the dock,
gnawing a blade of grass, the sun beginning to fleck

the wall of his house, whose single window a solitary
female figure leaned out of, unwilling to wave to him.

Courtship

A mere speck at first, the male eagle you've been watching
suddenly dives down on a female skimming the water past

the birches along the shore. You're in the lodge's old yellow
canoe, I'm in my pram fishing off your bow without any luck,

when suddenly you're pointing with your paddle, hollering so
I drop my rod to see what you see: the last second before he's

on her, she flips to her back so they can lock talons, roll over
and over till we grow dizzy. We lock grins before drifting apart

again, you to put in at a little cove, hunt for blueberries the bears
have missed, while I motor off to my best bass hole for the main

course of our nightly meal. For half a century we've come here
summers, up above the Canadian shield, as happy as we've ever

been, on the other side of rougher waters you've seen me through
than anything Loon Lake can toss up. If you ever need a tow back

now, the rope's coiled at my feet, though with your skills you play
the wind just right, are back at the dock when I putt-putt in.

Terminal Tackle

Which is everything that's attached
to the end of our line – leader, hook,
plug, sinker, fly or spoon. "If you rig it
right, there's a light inside," Hank says.

He's an elder at the reservation near
Lake Winnebago, guiding me now that
dad's dead, says he's good for one more
lesson on sturgeons' wily, wild ways.

"Don't try to understand what he means,
just watch what he does," dad whispered
when Hank showed me how to chop a proper
hole in the ice, which wouldn't slush up when

the spear flew out of dad's hand and Hank
whooped as the sturgeon cruising by slowed
down "to the speed limit." I can still hear him
yelling, "Let him run, let him run goddamnit!"

I'd be lying if I said that Hank took matters
into his own huge hands when I didn't coil
the rope right the spear was attached to, or
we spotted a few shadows under the oily

surface, but no such luck. "What now, Hank?"
I finally said when the day was spent. "Seeing
as how I'm terminal too," he said from the bow,
"I'm in a great hurry to move. Row, man, row!"

Lake of the Ozarks

Long after my brother, on our annual
fishing trip, hooked my sister's head
and with his needle-nosed pliers ever
so gingerly removed the treble hooks
while I held her hand hard, mid-lake,
and we rowed the top of the water off,
rushed her to town for a tetanus shot,
the hallway of the hospital festooned
with dozens of lures, extracted from
people and their pets, little plaques
commemorating the occasion – "Sally
will never sit on this one again"—

we sit around a winter fire planning
our return to the back bay where we
came across so many gar I'd lie if I
tried to say exactly how many, lazing
under the surface in the sun's last rays
before they spooked us into trying to
hook them. Sis managed to raise one,
so young it easily wriggled free when
we came to our senses, stowed the gear,
sat on our hands, and stared at the ancient
fish seeming to fix us in their sights, too.

"A fish so tenacious of life," The Wise
Fisherman's Encyclopedia says, it may
exist in drying pools when other species
have long since expired. Indians waited
for their souls to depart before slicing
off their scales, hard as diamonds, to
use as arrowheads. "It is foolish to try
to take them by hook and line…" Tell
us about it, we groan, rubbing the backs

of our heads before climbing into our
sleeping bags after the brandy disappears,
and we raise a glass to the gar in the book.

Mother, Fishing

We'd fluke along, driven by
the way she worked the oars,
as if she owned the whole lake.

I've seen water good as dead
brought back to life with her
rowing. If I could, I'd work

every single day like that,
even Sundays, till everyone
would see that things were

right—I'm blurting, excuse
me, but she's dead now, one
year to this August day out

on High Lake. Will I ever see
the musky she was after till
the end, the kind of fish whose

flesh will not go from greater
to less, is even too strong for
gefilte fish? I've left the shore

behind, with the repose of
a mother who'd close her eyes
before she tied into one: Now

this is a whale of a fish, she
yelled, And it's moving in with
us, make room! She waved off

the net I fetched, settled back
on the torn cushion, whispered,
Before I took over your father

was doing all right, you know.
Now hand me the pliers, the hook's
gone down too far. No glory in that.

Bitter End

The inboard end of the rope, in my hand,
to be made fast to the bits, just before

paying out the anchor's line. Who doesn't
know that? But I waited too long, again…

The anchor's on the bottom now, the day's
a wash, gray as always on Loon Lake, so

I'm not going in after it. Sometimes,
for the sake of something to do, I dive

down to see what else is down there next
to all my anchors. Found an armchair once,

sat down, crossed my legs, pushed up
my goggles and made eyes at all the fish

I wasn't catching. Felt relieved a moment,
like when you decide not to do something

you've always loved doing. Time flushed
quickly, I didn't notice how late it was

before I ran out of air, which is another
sort of bitter end, if you can think about it.

The Titanic's Hold

—for Shimon

"No precious gems, no gold, no other such riches.
Just 1,963 bags of potatoes, 28 bags of sticks, 76
cases of dragon's blood, a plant resin; also orchids,
lace collars, sardines, mushrooms, a case of toothpaste,
not to forget a huge number of shelled walnuts, though
not enough alas to keep it afloat. Nor could the most
valuable commodity aboard, millions of dollars of
feathers: 40 cases of plumes for New York's milliners…"

Tell me what God punished the passengers for, then,
I ask my blind rabbi, while I pet his guide dog till he says,
"Please, not when she's working." We're walking along
the local reservoir's rim, where little toy boats set afloat
yesterday at a town-wide picnic still haven't decided to
sink. Some have their little decks awash with trinkets
tiny children's hands stowed aboard. Lately I've been
feeling God's about to punish me for disobeying Him,
which my rabbi knows before I do. "One may live
without father or mother, but not without God," he says,
yanking the dog's leash; she'd rather jump in for a swim
than listen to us two old farts, I hear myself thinking.

"So when will they stop diving down to explore the wreck,"
I say when we're back for hummus and crackers, a little glass
of kosher wine. "Not until the ship gives up its last shred of
goods, and Jonah comes out of a dark recess, stroking his red
beard, ordering them back up to the rest of their unholy lives."
My rabbi's winking in his fashion, "Good old Jonah, good boy!"

Absent Flag

Square blue, flown from your boat it means
you're not aboard, dad. Sometimes, just knowing

you're not there now is enough to quell most
memories, ones we've somehow lived through

before deciding to treat troubles with denials.
"Ash Breeze" comes to mind, just so you know

there's an apt expression for the commotion you'd
make rowing from one dead hole to the next when

our luck went bad. No wonder we never caught
that monster bass, after you released a dozen smallies

when I blurted out I could no longer stomach filleting
them to your grim satisfaction. "Enough already!"

I'd had to scream when you said "Let's just try one
more hole, under the waterfall." Complicit once more,

I admit, though if you'd mounted one more trophy fish
over the mantle, I'd, well, never mind, dear old dad…

So now I'm sentenced to just dreaming about you,
turning up everywhere in the damndest spots, shouting

more curses out over the world, as only you could curse,
till the hoar-frost feathered your mustache. When the lake

iced up, you'd say the devil would finally move on, so
if we chopped a few holes our luck would change. And

that the last son of every last father should have blood
on his hands for cleaning even the tiniest mess of fish.

Wash-Hole

Mostly we swam in the stream's one deep muddy ditch,
but some Catholic kids begged to be baptized there, till
Father Feite, a priest displaced in WW II, slipped and went
under for some scary minutes. When he shot back up, he
hollered something in Dutch, which didn't seem too holy,
his vintage grin swamping his ruddy face. Everything

would have been all right if a few parents hadn't questioned
his wisdom, trying his patience enough to request a transfer.
Father Sturm, his replacement, got the town to post the hole,
which of course led to some kids drowning there afterward.
The plaque with their names, and the name of one boy's dog,
has since been washed away in Lodi's ugly floods. I went back

last year to trace some memories. No one around could remember
their names, but the old barber said "Peggy was the kid's mutt's
name. I know because my pop sold it to his pop one winter, best
hunting hound this side of Madison." The sign on his wall said
"Flat-tops are free," in memory of the kids who lost their lives.
"Just a trim," I said. He tightened the smock around my neck.

The Amur River

—for Steven

Where tribal fishermen bait hooks with dog
to catch taimen, the so-called tiger of ichthyo-
fauna for size and ferocity, I tell my brother,
the best fisherman I know, hoping he'll say
"The hell with it, let's go right now, buddy."

He's killed all the smallmouth around for miles
in Oneida County, getting bored, reminds me pop
used to say how much can you eat, anyway?
I head for another beer for both of us, yawn
the way I do when he's listening but not quite

hooked, and up the ante: "And the Amur's kaliega's
the largest freshwater fish in the world, a kind of
sturgeon that can top two tons!" Which gets him to
boot up the p.c., Google the Amur area map, so I
back off a bit. Years have passed since he's been

my boat boy, the one thing that kept us really close.
I put on my glasses, my temples wet with sweat,
ask him whether we should drink a little more
before we decide, then slowly leave the room,
but like a bad actor turning in the door, it hits me

how old we look, how frightened, how we're stuck
where we are. "There are sure to be monsters in our
lake," he says, "if we live long enough to hook one."

"A Hideous Thing to Find in the Heart of a Continent"

So said Kipling, looking out midwinter
at thunderous, monster waves pounding
Lake Superior's shore, before he ran back

for more food & drink at the only watering
hole around for miles. His many-sidedness
amazing, he could nonetheless shed tears,

grow hysterical, occasionally convulse I read.
I'm from a town named after him, have this
thing about tracking him of late, I confess

to the ragged bartender pouring me bad rum,
convinced it was Kipling's drink to ward off
the shakes in the same sort of weather brewing

outside the cracked window, winds sowing
the waves with renewed fury. "Remember
the Edmund Fitzgerald? Kipling predicted

something like that would have to happen,"
I tell him, quoting Kipling's *From Sea to Sea*:
"The stronger the waves, the more individual

our fears." At the moment, I'm not in a mood
for something tragic or even extraordinary, older
now than Kipling ever got to be. "More rum, mate!"

Pesticating

Not a word in most dictionaries, but used around here
to mean just walking along with nowhere in mind, but
keeping an eye peeled in case the road ahead, studded

with wheel-ruts, weeping willows on both sides, turns
into a graveyard, something to grow melancholy about.
I shift from one leg to the other; something's plumping

into a stream in the distance. I can't help imagining how
they'll talk about me if I don't return. Must have read
more than half the people in the world have never been

in trouble, but another matter if they've been thankful.
It's later now, the sun's skipped out of sight, so the stream
goes out like a dying ember. Suddenly my father's hearty

appetite comes to mind. He'd cut himself the biggest piece
of carp, scrape it with his knife, motion me to pour him
another beer. We'd been fishing together for the last time.

"I'm ordering you: put me into the cheapest wooden coffin,"
he'd say staring at the wall. "Set me off in our old rowboat,
shoot a flaming arrow into the side and watch me burn. What's

the matter with you?" Gritting my teeth, choking, I pointed
to his beer. He slid the glass down to my end of the table.
Before I could grab it, it slid back, as if a big ship lurched,

sending it back again. I'm down on the ground now, right
next to his marker. The caretaker raking leaves comes over,
"You all right, pal?" On my honor, I cannot swear I am.

Job's Tears

What some south of here call spiderwort,
its flowers in the early afternoon slowly turn
into teardrops. Once, coming through your

garden with a tired step, I found you crying
again, which you denied. "I'm just in clouds
is all, trying to see through to a safe landing."

I tried to say nothing at all, maintain a manly
face as always. You'd been affected much more
than I by what had happened. What a strange

thing the habit of dying is. "A child may die
without any intention of doing so," you said,
swaying from side to side. Like a plow cutting

the earth, I'd planted my anger as if there were
no other remedy, while you fought off temptation
to think nothing had happened yet. Trust was only

a matter of imagining. You seemed relieved when
I went away, praying as if from some distant
memory, the bible open on your lap, then dove
into the pond, your breath bubbling up from below.

Ithuriel's Spear

Common on hillsides, its flowers
like purple funnels. Harks back

to the angel dispatched to watch
over Adam and Eve. Seems to have

disappeared then, till the 16th
century, when Milton mistakenly

called it a cherub, who spotting
a toad touched it with its spear:

Lo, behold, Satan stepped forth!
Then, unaccountably, nothing till

WW I, when it became a British sub
in name till calamity struck (another tale).

Recently declared to help curb all
our lusts, for even if you're honorable,

seed life into all the fields around,
which animate, raise themselves, spread

shoulders out more and more come spring,
you're still nothing more than a lying devil

like all us other humans, in serious need
of a tender touch. Come on down, Ithuriel!

Meat-in-the-Pot

What dad called his twelve-gauge,
which he'd grab and make for some
woods when he'd had it up to here
with store-bought meat. We were
better off than the year before
when the Depression had us in its
pockets, but not a reason dad would
sign onto for bringing back some
venison, the occasional woodchuck,
hare for jugging. He'd serve himself
first, but expect me to "eat like a man."
I tried to stop looking queasy, never
shook my head, but my insides would
turn, I'd grow feverish, get the shakes.
He'd try calming me under the hose,
but when I began hyperventilating,
he'd get the sack to breathe into,
clench his fists. From such a son
a man might expect little if anything,
I saw him think, then drink some more.

Third & Galena

—in memory of Herb Blau

The Italians were Dagos, the French Frogs,
we were plain old Yids, and the Polish Umpkes
supplied us all with their cabbage rolls stuffed
with meat and rice, especially Augie's mom's.

After he'd muss me up for stealing just a pack
of Wings from my pop's drugstore, he'd let me
have a drag and touch the Capt. Richard Bong
card from the back of the pack, claiming he was

our first Ace of Polish descent, and you wouldn't
want to disagree, so I got to eat over at his house
again, where we'd polish off galumpkis as if they
were so many Twinkies and Mrs. Malowski sent

me home with a dozen more. Augie's dead & gone
now, so there's no reason to attend another reunion,
the only times I could beat him at arm wrestling. He
knew by then Bong was of Swedish descent, but I

didn't rub it in. After too many brews, we'd slip out
into the alley behind school, walk into the hollyhock
patch, pull out Camels, poor cousins of Wings, we
joked. Augie still carried Bong's card in his wallet,

whom we'd salute before heading back for the last of
the festivities, at which point the emcee, usually Freddie
Friedman, would have the spotlight directed at us, shout,
"There's America for you, folks, a Yid and an Umpke,

still friends no matter what!" Augie started coughing,
and I'd join him for solidarity until his lungs stopped
working, he'd stagger, all grew dark, something fell,
and the Chinese lanterns couldn't keep the light alive.

Gone to Sleep

What your feet do, more and more lately.
Moderately severe peripheral neuropathy,
all the tests confirmed. Could get worse,
medicate when necessary, but mostly try
to ignore till it lets loose a hive of angry
bees, then will your way past the buzzing
up and down both legs. The drama will pass.
Won't have to jump out the window yet,
just enough for wondering if you're foolish
enough to care so much for the word "dignity"
anymore, but let's talk about something else
now, please! Say the Bette Davis festival on
Bravo tonight – from Baby Jane on back to
the early career. I'll make the popcorn, you
open the beers.
                                My God, look at that face!
The same one she wore on Johnny Carson's
last year, twisted into a scowl after an ugly
stroke. "What was it like?" Johnny said gently.
"Getting old ain't for sissies, Johnny," she said.

2

Shedding Thoughts

Hallux

The reversed toe that lets perching birds
grip a branch, I read. Would the plural be

halices, I ask my funny old high school
Latin teacher in a dream, whom we said

awful things about in recess. Her eyes flash,
she raises her hands to her head, straightening

her hair, removing something like a knitting
needle to point at our stupid faces, "Ah, you

miserable prisoners!" Her admonishing finger
gets me to her side quicker than I know I can run.

"When I leave you to your empty devices, void
and desolate of counsel," she sinks into a reverie,

"I take several streetcars and one bus, until I am
back with my peregrine falcon at my farmhouse.

If you don't fail me, I shall let you pet him some day,
before I send him sky-high so he can show you why

he's the fastest bird in the skies." She kept me by
the force of her grip from thinking anything but.

Water Ouzel

Go after cutthroat, Dolly Varden or
other mountain trout if you want to

spot one. For unknown reasons, it's
usually right there, on a bulge of rock,

midstream, dipping up and down,
building a nest of green mosses

in tangled tree roots the water
courses through. Toward dusk,

it flies in and out of the ripples,
hunting roe, water walkers, beetles.

Once, right before a trout hit, I
broke off casting just to watch it,

the ouzel staring at me, bewildered,
breathing hard, a porous respect for

other meanings perhaps: Shakespeare
came to mind, but the ouzel beat me

to him: "Forget that crock," it lisped,
"About 'the woosell cocke, so blacke

of hew, with orange-tawny bill,' pal.
He never saw one of us in all his life."

Cleptoparisitic

behavior's what they call one bird snatching
another's catch midair, at which frigates excel.

As if taking a dip in cold water on a hot day,
the one we're watching is ruffling as it climbs,

its beak glistening, inducing momentary vertigo,
so you brace your leg against mine to stop my

wobble. My mind goes dumb; "too much white
plaque," Dr. Wu noted, who scanned the MRI,

"foresee a possibility of MS." How to relax after
that news, I asked him. "Go Galapagos, see some

ancient animals" was all he needed to prescribe,
so here we are, but it's just some sort of pretense,

I realize, thinking more and more of what we've
been saying more and more: Please God, let me

go first... The frigate lands nearby, and you point
to its quick movements biting through the fish as

it flops, bristling with each surgical slice, before
sharpening its beak on a stone. "No, no, don't want

any solemn promises, you won't fail me, will you?"
You kneel down, look the frigate in the eye. "What's

the cliché, there are lots of good fish in the sea, but
stealing from one of your kind's close to drawing

a curtain back to see the Devil's face?" Warned it's
too early to be here to see much mating, we take time

for one of our huge hugs, veins in my throat swelling.
As if on cue, you start laughing to my heart's content,

so I finally sense there's no earthly use crying over spilt
plaque, which only lasts as long as a good sauce takes.

Birds of Paradise

Early specimens shipped from the Moluccas,
to satisfy European appetites for anything new
under the sun of creation, seemed to have no feet;

hence they must always be aloft, some fanciful
theorists concluded, who might have known better.
The cruel truth: their legs had been cut off for easy

shipping. We no longer wonder at such acts though
they repulse us, while the mind's restless eye contorts:
why, the females lay eggs in holes on males' backs!

Just one more myriad flight of fancy, till Darwin's nemesis,
Alfred Russell Wallace, brought back the first two so-called
Lesser Birds alive, which we call sempioptera wallaceii today.

No moral in the end, except perhaps that God made both men
with no need to work, but such creatures for their hearts heavy
with losses over children, their competitive urges withering.

Tucotuco

The mole-like creatures with the onomatopoetic name,
which brought Darwin to his knees to give a listen with
his good ear to the sound it emits from its tunnel, its huge
eye barely rudimentary, virtually useless, or so some think.

With a cold shiver down my back, I've asked the very same
question of my mind's eye: why so big and yet so empty-
headed, at best reminding me of former prosperity, but also
present sorrow, which precipitates melancholy known only

to very old souls, assuming I have one? Today's passing
in peculiar stillness and languor, brooding as I have been
about Darwin's failure to explain that eye away. "As if it
were his fault?" my mother thumps from about the same

distance belowground the tucotuco knows like the top of
its grubby snout. Darwin first grows quiet listening, then
begins to laugh. Mother's silent of course, but the wood
around her's crumbling, and if she spoke she'd say, "Go

to sleep, Charles. You've eaten, drunk, must be so sleepy.
Not to worry, I'll keep the Tuc around somehow. What claws
he has, got to roll out of the way now!" A stupefied look
in his eyes, he'd say, "Great thanks, Gert. My whole future,

all my plans, everything hinges on it!" Time for me to
sing both their praises, throw in a chorus for the tucotuco.
Even the dead can't be fed on fairy-tales, so I warble a Te
Deum, begin to dig my own tunnel with a chip of wood.

Tom, Dick & Harry

The only live specimens the Beagle brought back
to England: the three baby tortoises Darwin named

in his affectionate way were installed as family pets
at first, till they turned to eating more and more and

soon reached sizes large enough to reveal Harry was
female, and promptly renamed him Harriet, who died

not so long ago on a farm down under, a friend having
persuaded the Darwins to let her have a longer life after

scientific curiosities were satisfied. Few mammals can
outlive tortoises, but their current fate greatly troubles

the mind, given their loss of habitat, our often misguided
tenderness, and a black market trade that rivals any other

creature's current fate. Darwin, who I read would drop
everything to scratch their throats and help them up into

his lap, was also trying to learn what sort of man he was,
even as he filled notebooks daily with his observations.

Smelling of perspiration, he'd stare into their eyes, gather
his children around and shout, "Come, let us drink a glass

to hearts of beasts, Dearies," the tortoises hissing in chorus.
They hardly had time to crawl an inch before the children

rushed outside to play "Tom, Dick & Harry," their version
of behaving naturally. It was pure impulse and unaccountable.

Sea Squirt

Can you believe we're related? Not only that!
Their vital organs, I read, are "protected by

a layer of special connective tissue – *mesenchyme*—
which turns up in human embryos." Best of all,

for us these days, they harbor the secret of how
to re-grow tissue. You say that's of little interest?

You'd better come nearer so we can have a chat
about something. A light shines on the spot where

we're lost to the rest of the night. In the morning,
we begin to live a different life, which invests us

with a certain air among friends, who do not know
you need a transplant, and of course I never whisper

a word about it, which you consider an act of kindness.
When I suggest a trip to the aquarium, you say okay but

no fine talk. Pressing up against the glass, hoping they'll
detach from their rocks, reattach to your palm imprints,

you whisper, "Now I'll have the transplant; and then, God
willing, back to more life, without which we're dead you

said, remember?" I'll make myself eat the glass, I think,
choke back my fear. She'll die, the Devil whispers in

my ear. "Why are you crossing yourself?" she says. "You're
not a believer." "Yes, yes, I know," I stammer. "I'm just

thirsty is all, and asking God for a little vial of pure hope."
Your laugh's nothing but the pure, crystalline key of C.

Hammerheads

The shark's better known perhaps, but the bat
deserves some respect, too! I read males have

huge heads, which are quite hollow, oversized
lips and the biggest larynx for their size of most

mammals, so when they sing females flying by
have a hard time deciding whose tune they prefer

for all the cacophony. When you see one, the woman
researcher I've been reading says, "You want to don

a hat with silk ribbons and a midnight-black flowered
shawl." I should be so lucky, who've only netted brown

bats in my lifetime that edged through the cracks in our
red brick walls, though I did come close to being bitten

back at school, the long curving promenade up to my dorm
along Lake Mendota flooded nights by daunting swarms of

the local species. In those dreary days, I was straying into
German studies, against my gramma's pleas: "Don't devote

any more time to the language of the enemy," she'd say, even
on her death bed. I'd protest, meekly quote some Rilke, which

she'd counter with a bolus of Pushkin poems. "And besides,"
she always got in before I kissed her goodbye, "By now you

could be at least a colonel in the armed forces if I'd hammered
all the Russian I know into you." I drink to the image of the bat

in the book, drink some more to Pushkin's picture on the wall
over gramma's bed, drink till I edge through the new cracks.

Meerkat

Hard to believe, but have on good authority
"they teach their young but one thing: how
to eat poisonous scorpions without getting
stung." The one I'm watching inside its cage
folds its paws, leans back as if in an easy chair:
"A good creature, sir, which does not repulse,"
the man trying to sell it says, "so easy to train
as a pet, will keep scorpions from your slippers
when you wake up. It's a good price for you,
and a good price for me, sir." I'd be tempted
if he knew why it's so-called. We are not near
the sea, and while the left side of my brain thinks
it's cat-like, the right rejects that conclusion; and
the thalamus throws in a sense of shame and guilt.
(My frontal lobe finally lights up: you're playing
some sort of game with the Devil!) I am sorry for it,
I stammer to its owner, but it's a lie; and move away
to the next stall, the air heavy with a sullen silence.

Suddenly the meerkat man comes flying after me,
seizes my jacket: "What sort of man are you? You
must rescue the poor animal, and me from having
to sell it!" Two hours later I knock at my wife's
door: "My eyes have been opened, Love, I pray
you understand me." She says she is ready to hear
anything I have to say, fit or unfit for her to hear,
while she extends an arm to the meerkat, which
takes to it like a branch from its favorite tree.

Milk Snake

Speckled like a rattler, but it's harmless enough.
You swear you saw one climb a cow's leg once,
coil around it, and suck away at a teat it could
barely reach. Old wives' tale – I try to calm you,
watching you nurse our first born. She wants
more ninny, you croon, when you both wake up
from a little doze. Along the sky stars poke out,
casting their light for the night. Out from baby's
cap, dark curls fall over her brow. Her thumb's
stuck in your bra, her belly's filling with milk,
the rocker's creaking, the pine planks spreading,
till the whole room yearns for better things, and
you cry, shedding your fright. Off you go, lowest
of the low, slither into the garden of less delight!

Spiders in Winter

Make for our cellar weather.
I used to suck them up into

the silky soft bag of the Black
& Decker shop-vac, watch them

slowly stretch back to life after
I slit them out in spring, but now

in my likely last decade I glass
them in an old terrarium where

they seem to shiver, turning heads
this way and that as I sing to them

in my weak baritone, Praise God,
from whom all blessings flow; lift

my shot-glass from the workbench,
knock back a few schnapps, bow,

touching a kiss to the wolf spider's
nose on the other side of the glass,

her babies alight on her hairy back.
She's my dearest specimen, scared

me before I Googled her: fierce to be
sure, possibly poisonous, but only if

threatened. There's that word again—
an indication of something impending.

Cougars Kill People

But prefer children, I say, killing the usual family gossip
—who's on or off the wagon again, who's bi-polaring, not
taking meds on schedule, losing tons in the market – we're
at the annual Thanksgiving get-together at Aunt Jessie's.
But we all have kids, one thing we still have in common.

Uncle Oliver finally says, spinning the ice in his glass,
"Where?" Like an echo, I say, "Where?" "You're in one
of your melancholy moods again," Aunt Bea says, "Keep
it up and you'll drive me to drink even more." "We're not
at the point yet of having drunk enough to stupefy us,"

Cousin Ethel tosses over her shoulder, on the way for
a refill. Leaning against the bookcase, Gramma Anna
suddenly opens what looks like a bible. "For those whose
hands are defiled by blood, Isaiah lix. 2-11," she warbles.
Distant cousin Max, down from the U.P., demands I

supply the exact reference, starts yelling I read too many
books for bits to interject when I don't like the drift, jumps
up from the couch, sticks his jaw into mine. He's a big man,
with an unhealthy complexion, a milkman who once found
me under his horse and slapped the hell out of me. No one

was in time to stop him. As for me, I'm beginning to forget
where I read most anything, think I might even be making
it all up. And think of running away when I blabber things.
Well, there we all are, waiting for Grampa Izzie to die in
the back bedroom, so we can put a clove in his hairy nose.

He's the only one of us who's ever seen anything remotely
like a cougar, somewhere in the Carpathians, on his way to
a boat in London that would land at Ellis Island in 1910, and
quickly got out of its way when it leapt out of the woods. He'd
act out both parts when we were impressionable, and begged.

Surplus Killing

Said to be triggered by "easy meat," animals
caught in deep snow, say, or vulnerable young.

Wolves, bears, lions and tigers, hormones flooding
their blood, can't help themselves, kill so quickly

if you blink you miss the next take-down, their faces
heavy with the color of raw meat. "Drink some water,"

our guide says. "That will calm you." He leads us to
the most secluded corner of the quadrant. We learn

that what the ravens and eagles don't get is donated
to soup kitchens. "I'd be curious to see the faces of

those who believe in nothing after witnessing a kill,"
I sputter before I'm sorry for the thought. One day,

after returning home, there's a letter on the table:
"Yes, I must write you," it says. "No longer guiding.

Had an awful time in your company." Minutes pass
before I realize he's written just to me. I said a lot

of other thoughtless things without thinking that day.

Beast of Kings

Not the lion guarding Ramses II's tent at night,
not Scimitar, Marcus Aurelius' companion at table,

while others explored the bed chambers of besotted
guests, not even the lion on Jerusalem's escutcheon,

the one I brood about while waiting to hear if a friend's
died in the recent bus attack. Certainly not the one Pope

what's-his-name sent to Charlemagne, nor the grizzled
one guarding the Tower of London, which could smell

a virgin among the throngs, and never mind the first one
to arrive in America in 1776. The one I have in mind on

this "Gloomy Sunday," playing the song over and over
that sent some leaping to their deaths in the Depression,

is a comical cartoon character, so good-natured the cooks
are butchering a herd of goats and roasting them instead.

Everything Else

being normal, when elephants
wear down their massive molars,

can no longer chew, they mostly
die, which takes about as long as

humans take to do so. My mother
loved keeping elephants at the zoo

company till closing time, false teeth
granting her a few bonus years. "Please

take them out now," she said with a last
breath, "and put them in the martini cup

in the drawer." Her granddaughter, more
in the moment, had not forgotten mother's

plea for a "memorial martini," made sure
we stopped at a bar around the corner from

the nursing home. That murderous August
week no elephants at the zoo were allowed

out of their quarters into the searing heat.
I tried a few disarming remarks, thinking

there was nothing else to be done, trying
not to paint the picture of misery, when

my daughter gently pushed me closer to
my mother's pillow. Like a baby elephant

nudging its trunk behind its mother's huge
ear, I snugged up under my dying mother's.

Suddenly frantic, she turned aside, pointing
a trembling finger at her open mouth till we

realized we'd forgotten to remove her teeth!
My daughter on one side, I on the other, we

tugged and tugged as mercifully as possible
around the gum line but nothing budged. "Is

this what you're looking for?" a nurse poking
her head in said. "I took them by mistake…"

Stotting

Vigorously jumping up & down, as if
on a Pogo stick, sometimes referred to

as pronking: what animals like moose,
elk or deer will do to monitor predator

movements. If you're close, you'd best
not say a word if you don't want to be

plowed under when they start to run—
but if you're dying, they'll quiet down,

return to browsing, pass on to another
spot, then a third, till at last you'll find

yourself past your own last struggle.

3

Not Everything's Always Clear

Flying Wedding Rings

"Slung beneath retired Wellington bombers," I read,
"huge coils were wound around a steel core," through
which powerful currents built up magnetic fields to

trip sensors of enemy mines in the deadly waters below,
the planes struggling to climb or, luckless, surging plumes
would bring them down. Not a happy trade-off, Churchill

growled, twisting his wedding ring, stamping out his cigar.
Once I tried to smoke as many in a day as he till Doc Wulff
pointed to some dark spots on the X-ray, started me twisting

my wedding band instead whenever I got the urge to light up,
which sent me back to the middle of Lake Gogebic on a stormy
honeymoon outing. Giddy about our finally tying an old knot,

my wife threw up her hands: "My ring just fits!" The moment
after it flew off, she shouted louder, waiting for me to dive in
after it. Afraid to admit I couldn't swim, hemming and hawing,

I weighed anchor and rowed to shore in the silence of clichés.
Atop a sandbar, in just three feet of water, we learned later, has
led to other silences. I've ceased claiming the water was muddy

enough to hide anything, never mention reading anything about
what's below the surface of any body of water, just surf channels,
dying to know how long the current wars will last, afraid to swim.

Sow Cat

As often as not, my Hungarian grampa would pat his lap
and chortle, "Come to me, you little *Schmendrick*," while
my Czech gramma would coo from the other Biedermeier
chair they'd schlepped along somehow from the old country,
"No, you better come to me, my little *sow cat*," but did not
want to talk about her past. Instead, grampa was in charge
of the main memories: head and shoulders above the rest,
how they met crossing the main bridge over the Danube in
Budapest when she left Senice for work as a domestic and
happened to drop her handkerchief, which of course he just
happened to pick up. But I begged for the tale of the architect,
who, when he realized one of the lions at bridge end lacked
a tongue, jumped into the river and drowned. Grampa kept
flailing his one good arm, grazing my head, while he went
on about hiding in fields of huge sunflowers to escape military
service, marching right behind Louie Kossuth in that fateful
parade that turned out the riot police with truncheons, until
Gramma groused, "Enough now, it's time for some strudel."
I sprinted after her like a traitor to the bosom of her kitchen,
off limits to anyone from Hungary, whose nose grew as he
babbled on about the glories of the Austro-Hungarian Empire.

Golden Bees

Gramma used to contend would halo
my head but not sting because the imp

in me would pin them to the cork board
on my wall, even as I cried out for alcohol

to blot the welt. "He'll be a great coleopterist,"
she'd tell anyone passing by, "unless he becomes

a Nazi hunter too like what's-his-name who just
died, or maybe write novels on the side like that

crazy Russian who wrote filth when he ran out
of breath chasing butterflies. God keep him in

Purgatory till… Now where was I?" she'd stammer
when Grampa came back from tending hives down

by the creek on their scrubby patch in Little Vilna,
aka Lodi, Wisconsin, where the honey they harvested

put a foolish look called lunacy on your face if you
ate too much. Here I am now, an old soul at eighty,

confessing I've become nothing of the above, just mull
missed opportunities, waiting for word from other imps
of having ruined their chances of making reparations.

Brief Reflection on Weapons

"The more murderous the weapon,
the gentler its name," I read; to wit,
Big Bertha & Kutyusha (a Russian
heroine), those two formidable cannon;
Scavenger's Daughter (a device to compress
the body into hemorrhaging); *The Lazy Grete,*
Long Tom, Brown Bess, Mons Meg, and
Just plain *Gun*, perhaps from Gunilda…

"If you learn to shoot as I teach you to, I'll
give you food and shelter," my father said,
handing me his twelve-gauge to oil and clean.
I only saw him smile when mother gave him
supper, warmed up for when he trudged home
from work. She always put aside the best cuts.
People say the way he chewed would turn heads.
I apologized to every one of them for failing him.

Hopeful when I finally put a shot in the outer ring,
straw bursting from the plump target, he suddenly
spoke in a strange voice: "One day I won't be here,
you'll look here and there, no father. But with this
gun, something passing between us to draw us close…"
He shut his eyes, put his hands on my shoulders, nails
broken, fingers worn, hands that sometimes twined
around my neck: "A weapon can't understand a thing,

how the air vibrates, what's going on in your head." He
finished off the last shot, my cue to track spent shells while
he wiped the gun one end to the other with a soiled cloth.

"Large Sturgeon Caught with Iron Cross in Its Stomach"

So ran a headline in 1927: turns out
a WW I German soldier, despondent,
jumped into a river and drowned.

No one took notice of the fisherman,
a long-gone cousin of Erich, my best
pal from exchange-students days in

Germany, who rigged the cross and
ribbon up as some sort of metronome
to practice piano by. Turning his score's

pages, I'd sit beside him till his mother
called us to raspberries & cream. She'd
steer us around "shameful thoughts" of

the war with such tenderness we'd stop
short of darker worries. "That was our way,"
she'd always end up saying, "But not God's."
Having translated German poets for years,
who didn't choose exile, who may have
"contributed," the Commissions put it, I

only know I'd also have taken fright and
not drawn myself up to my full height in
like circumstances. Would you have, well?

Crook-Nose Jack McCall

Hanged, we're certain, for shooting
Wild Bill Hickok back of the head.

Remember Calamity Jane sobbing away
in that movie kids my age went to in droves

in the 30s? I wanted to change my name
legally, but my mother said we couldn't

afford it. "Besides," she said, 'Crook-nose
Stu doesn't drink yet, or jump his pals from

behind." When I started to fool around with
a rope, practiced jumping off the kitchen stool,

eyeing the ceiling for a place to secure a knot,
my father finally hollered, "Enough!" As if I

were a killer who'd murder his victims for
their gold. I ran out the back door and didn't

stop till I came to some woods, a cloud of smoke
rising from a hollow, where an old man sat,

cooking something strange on a spit. "It's
not the way I used to live, kid, before I shot

my best friend." Tracing my nose with
a swollen finger, he snarled: "You next?

Not hardly, kid, not till you can shoot
straight, cinch a knot that won't slip."

"Lonesome Charley"

Had a premonition that he'd die in
the morning, right by Custer's side,

so he gave away all he owned, even
his Bowie knife. For unknown reasons,

he seemed ashamed of me in a dream,
even a little angry about something.

"Are we ever to have an end of this?"
I kept pleading. "Shut the hell up,"

he said, rubbing his face red with his
neckerchief. "Besides, the Big Horn's

an imbecile place to be at this point in
my stupid life, but start shedding blood

it's hard to stop." His horse died before
he did, the book says, and the epaulettes

stuck to his shoulders when he tried
to peel them off before splashing into

the muddy sward like a pig. I pulled
on my boots, got right down beside him,

dragged him to a dry spot, and lifted
his head till the wrinkles left his face.

A Wrestler Named Plato

Not the bum we hollered at on the south side
of Chicago, who'd twist the other bum's head
between the ropes till he miraculously extricated
himself and stomped on the first bum's back like
a jumping jack till the ref somehow yanked them
apart. When he winked, dad yelled for our money
back till the guys behind us hissed, "Shut the damn
fuck up!"; and pushed dad down. I tried not to cry.

I mean Socrates' buddy of sorts, whose gymnastics
coach called him *Platon*, "broad-shouldered," and I
bet got him more than ready for the Isthmian Games.
No one seems to know how he fared, but I've been
examining my grimy copy of his writings for hints &
hidden clues to some avail: by the laws of his body
he must have gotten in some mighty kicks, dropping
at least one opponent in the dust at his feet before he
was taught a lesson in return. Later, Socrates did his
part to remind him of man's weakness. No humbug
about him who said, "Enough now, no need to recall
the past. The bleeding's stopped. Your wounds are not
serious." Then they engaged in another loud argument.

Love of Science

Leonardo ran breathless to the convent,
climbed the scaffold, painted till dawn
faded, no food or rest in sight. Then,
inexplicably, for a number of days he
wouldn't go near the place, just locked
himself in with dangerous reptiles to
observe their habits, or took to Milano
streets, searching for a face vile enough
to model for Judas, or drank with drunks
to study the expressions they assumed. So
how come he was so careless mixing oils,
which soon faded? Love of science, some
say, drove him to those foolish experiments.

"Forget *The Last Supper*," I said to Raboni,
who'd arranged for us to be present while it
was undergoing restoration, "What I fear's
the wall turning blacker in that red chalk
drawing of *The Battle of Anghiari*, so can
we hurry on to Turin before it vanishes?"

Precipitazione Dall'alto

Fall from a high place, that is, as noted in
official documents, which brings to mind

Primo Levi's death in spades and clubs. After
dinner we hurry to see the stairwell he jumped

into, or fell as some have posited. Looking
up, we wish him still standing behind the low

banister, not sure what to do next, frozen by
remorse if that's what engulfed him; but he's

not. For a quarter of a century now, we've tried
living as quietly and peacefully as possible, you

attending Mass wherever available, I thinking
about converting, much more impatient, a vile

image coming over me at times, clenching fists
now and then, rarely able to keep my muttering

private. "Come," you manage to shake me free,
"Let's drink something to his memory, decide to

donate our bodies to research," which means of
course we must not suffer a violent death, the form

warns, or die of something communicable. Reading
the fine print, I stammer: "One may donate one's eyes,

but nothing else," and hand over the clinic's manual.
"That'll do for now," you whisper, "if not end the tale."

"A Single Quantum of Visible Light"

Has only about a trillionth the energy
of a fly's wing-beat, imagine! Flies on my

window are all eyes, which also deserves
astonishment if not admiration, or are such

thoughts a gift of this illness: trembling,
saying nothing while on the other side

of the window the grass is up to waists,
trees under attack from hitherto unknown

beetles stabbing to their hearts. They do
not sing; they merely munch. Talk about

quantum energy we still can't comprehend!
Not even Dirac or Heisenberg or, gulp and

gasp, Einstein couldn't help but tumble along
the way to any understanding. The century of

"a man's capable of understanding anything"
had long since twitched its whiskers looking

through microscopes at little violet specks, or
were they just agitated negative space colored

by the fancy of Einstein's cunning *Herr Gott*?
"If He were truly angry, the best way to keep

vows and do His will," Einstein wrote to Bohr,
"would be to stay the fool and go on plowing."

Spaghettification

Get close enough to a black hole,
the books all say, you'll be torn to
shreds before learning anything

about time's flow. Tossing side to
side I boil some pasta, lick the bowl
clean, then curl up and fall asleep

till Einstein comes calling. Let us go
and drink, he says, breathing rapidly,
his face sunken, so I sigh and take him

by both hands. Yes, I have worries too,
I try to soothe him, Especially about my
grandson, who's so young I won't be

around to watch him take on his world.
See that dead star up there? Einstein's
finger is crooked, arthritic, so I can't see

what he does, not to mention I'm so used
to thinking everything happens mostly in
books. He cuts me short, Is your grandson

OK for now? Thank God, yes, I almost shout.
Well then, let me worry about odd pieces of
information. Do you happen to like borscht?

Supraoral

Lying above, not with a mouth.
A strange word, I thought, lying

in the sleeping bag, in which my
dad died out hunting bear, when he

should have been otherwise occupied.
Or that's what mom said, sitting down

after the viewing, her eyes darker than
usual. He'd never shaved his mustache

off, even when his customers said aloud,
"Why would you want to remind us of

Hitler?" Bored with business, one day he
just locked the door to his drugstore, back

in Lodi, and muttered he was finally going
to get the lone bear his yearly permit allowed.

We thought he was just sticking it to mom, who
shrieked "divorce" if he even thought so much

as having it stuffed, standing it in the window.
"Be my best goddamn display ever," he said so

darkly my sister and I choked on those words.
I'm out in the same sort of brutal weather he

lost his life in, something about honoring his
memory I don't understand myself. At first, I

tried growing the same little brush of mustache,
till my brother said, "Why would even a Jew in

name only want to do that, you jerk!" He'd never
read *Fathers and Sons*, so I just ignored him.

"Meanwhile, Bazarov was not altogether mistaken"
(p. 107). It's my umpteenth time through the woods.

Brief Reflection on the Black 6 Mouse

One dreary Prague morning, everyone wall-eyed,
Russian tanks still circling the crumbling Clinic

for Experimental Medicine, Dr. Holub, as I'd
call him in those difficult days, introduced me

to his "silly poetic pals," he joked in his way –
a special strain of nude mice, which his Russian

assistant, who'd often forget to wash her hands,
doom ongoing experiments, padded in with—

a new generation in their little tray, buried under
wood-shavings, dozens of beady eyes protruding.

Fingering a tail, he pulled one up, swung it back
& forth, and put it on my arm before coaxing it

down into his palm, reminding me of my Russian
grandmother making a mouse from a big kerchief,

popping it along her arm by flexing her muscles.
I felt its skin, rubbery like a rhino's I once touched.

Then it hit: where is the fur!? Incredible, something
we know by one skin, in another. Something so fetal

I looked around for a tube to slide it in. When Dr. Holub
was called to the phone, his assistant left me with the tray.

As if my life depended on it, I fed the whole lot tidbits
from a jar, providing like a mother. "What do you think
you are doing, feeding them unsterile food? It will ruin

our data," Dr. Holub shouted when he returned, which
brought his assistant running too. "But Professor," her

voice dimming, "What difference does it make? No one
cares anymore…" His head drooped. "Well, then, you might

as well pet them too," he said. "Let's go try to see Kafka's
grave now, he'll be eager to know all's quite normal still.

But first let's repair to the Zlata Studna for some Pilsner
to toast 'normality.' Long may we pretend not to need it!"

he sang, brushing crumbs from table to floor for a black
mouse whiskering by. After tipping back a few brews, we

spoke more cheerfully, if little from then on to the end of
my first of many stays, resting heads on hands till closing.

Seeing the Elephant

First read D. H. Lawrence's *Elephant*
to set one memory-peg, Teddy's *African*
Game Trails for the other; not to mention
Nietzsche for an overview, so we can join
forces to bring the old expression back alive.

Some would prefer the lion or whale simile,
given that most humans still don't encounter
them in the wilds much, but I'm with Teddy:
"It is the most interesting of animals," hence
stands the best chance of getting your attention

when something you have witnessed, elbowing
your way through more and more horrors of late,
bangs your fist on the table, beside yourself with
rage to spread your fright, even if just eliciting
"What's the matter, dear?" from your mother,

who will quickly follow you to your study, her
robe gliding behind her. When you drop down
before the holy picture askew on the wall, she
straightens it with her cane, muttering to herself,
shaking her head before she says, "We must look

at things more simply. If there's food, good; if not,
bad, and then stop: where will it get you?" You bolt
past her out to the yard, dig a hole while she watches
at the window. Still afraid of what you've seen, that
day in Yad Vashem, you find some mettle to dig on.

"Two Great Minds Afloat"

—Gordon Fraser, The Quantum Exodus

Decent sailors by all reports, Schrödinger and Einstein
got in some R&R in their Berlin days together eddying

around on Berlin's outlying lakes before skies darkened
by Nazi doings sent them off to other waters to the west.

In the only picture they're so tiny it makes you laugh to
look at them, their bright eyes ablaze as if they understand

everything. One has no business there, but the other might,
you think, what with more and more records getting vetted.

Alas, no one else was aboard to report their conversations
except for a cat curled under the jibboom. Perhaps they just

talked about domestic matters – we know women sometimes
preoccupied them. Perhaps just about the wind and waves,

which might have led to equations if they had a blackboard.
At any rate, there were no scandals on the horizon yet. Look

how alone they are in their laughter! Do they want us to open
another beer, shout things like "we never expected you to…"?

Time to turn the page, leave them to their heavens, all smeared
with dark now to the mind's eye. Not everything's always clear.

Kornjuden

What Jews accused of raising grain prices in Germany
in 1816 were called, "the year without summer," I read.
So what else is new? The old man ate his gruel, the old
woman licked her bowl clean, but only after she ground
her teeth and he clenched his fists, while we sometimes
still cry, our faith no answer for much of anything these
dreary days absent peace among the usual adversaries.

Time for less silence, our Israeli cousins finally wrote,
along with a tinny CD of their youngest practicing to play
like Horowitz, they joked. When I knocked after decades of
of nothing between us, our common language German
because I bailed out of Hebrew school and their Yiddish
could morph into German between deep breaths, we sat
circled around little Esther, pecking away at the keys.

Abba Kovner, wired to everyone alive, made just two calls
via the Hebrew fragment on the "precious" postcard from
mom's long-lost cousins we thought murdered, which she'd
sent me off with to hunt for them. Cousin Max, Esther's father,
tipped his jigger to toast the coming rye harvest, the grain that
can poison you if it's not detoxified. We ate our fill, moving
from table to stove and back again all through the long night.

The Last Mattress

is starting to sink in the center, bad for the back as you know.
Which is why I am more sullen than usual these days, having

hoped I could avoid popping even more pills before I "catch
the cab," which lingo I have courtesy of my poet-pal on Death

Row, who never complains about his mattress or back, though
of course about plenty else. I think I agreed to witness his being

"offed," which can happen most anytime now that the governor
just needs to pluck his name from the pile on his desk: the string's

run out on appeals. The Devil himself would high-ten the governor
if he did what he wanted. I've also found he'll do anything I desire

on occasion, have had close conversations some nights, neither
of us sleeping much. Once he left clutching his back in such pain

he muttered he could have gone out that second to his execution.
God says I should leave the Devil my mattress, work to revoke

the DP, and even if we keep to our beds for a while, some stretching
is all that's needed to right our back for other desperate attempts.

Death-Qualified

—for PZ & STB

If in Florida, summoned to jury duty, and say "yes"
loud enough for the prosecuting attorney, you're

legal to vote for the Death Penalty with the state's
blessing, and directed to take a seat in the back row

of the box. Memories of childhood no longer obtain,
it's the moment to rub your forehead. The accused

when you look wishes he could run away, his shaved
head on one of those bodies with one of those hands

that did not mean to take the apple. It's getting warmer
in the courtroom, no one wants to sit in judgment on

such a day, the ocean not that far away. You ask for
permission to remove your jacket and tie. "Denied!"

says the judge. Okay, then, what if I just slip off shoes,
you say to yourself. They'll never know. Besides, I'm

thirsty, a faithful, sober person with no intention of
doing wrong, and wouldn't like to be wronged in return.

"Ah, yes," the attorney says, but only to clear her throat.
If it be done may it be undone at once, you whisper to

no one in particular, your heel pounding the floor. Someone
shouts, "Abandon ship you mongrels before the waves invade!"

Supersedure

1

Under the notch in the old willow, home
of many a hive, I read workers kill the old

queen when a new queen emerges to mate,
one of only two ways the colony "requeens."

Swarming's the other m.o. : numbers of queens
are bred by being fed royal jelly, a protein-laden

glob the hypopharygeal gland in mature workers
exudes. I look up to clear my eyes, the meadow's

suddenly alive with a hovering swarm, so I put
my book down, quickly net my head, start running.

2

There's dead silence now; night's curtain's fallen.
I'd be lying if I said I caught up with the swarm to

return to for any honey the bees might share without
retribution. I'd just wanted to be somewhere else, no

more craving for conflict, knowledge of the efficient
world. My heart's slowing. Now when I cut off a twig

I don't cut the air with a swish, begin to break into words.
Really, I'd do anything you told me to if it didn't cause

trouble, begin chores hoping not to finish them; what would
spread out over less than a page. "Breathing's my hobby, man,"

an old friend on Death Row writes. No one's jokes are as rich.
I just hope I'll be the first to arrive if out of air at the last hive.

Stuart Friebert received a Ph.D. at U. Wisconsin—Madison in German Language & Literature in 1958. He taught at Mt. Holyoke College (1957-59), and Harvard University (1959-61), before settling at Oberlin College in 1961. With help from colleagues, he founded Oberlin's Creative Writing Program and directed it until retiring in 1997. He co-founded *Field Magazine*, and later, the Field Translation Series/Oberlin College Press.

He has published thirteen previous collections of poems. Among them, *Funeral Pie* co-won the Four Way Book Award in 1997, and *Floating Heart* won the Ohioana Book Award for poetry in 2015. He has also published ten volumes of translations. With David Young, he has co-edited two anthologies, *The Longman Anthology of Contemporary Poetry* and *Models of the Universe: An Anthology of the Prose Poem*. With David Young & David Walker, he co-edited *A Field Guide to Contemporary Poetry & Poetics*. He has also published a textbook edition of Max Frisch's *Als der Krieg zu Ende war*.

Having started to write prose in 2000, he has published a number of stories and memoir-pieces, which are collected in a volume entitled *The Language of the Enemy*, forthcoming from Black Mountain Press. He has also published numerous critical essays and reviews, held an N.E.A. Fellowship in poetry, and received a number of awards for poems and translations over the years.

CPSIA information can be obtained at www.ICGtesting.com
Printed in the USA
LVOW10s0712280715

447910LV00003B/7/P